# Daily Routine Makeover

## Guide To Focused Action

## Productivity Hacks

## Stress-Free Performance

## Get Things Done In Less Time

## By Zoe McKey

Communication Coach and Social Development Trainer

zoemckey@gmail.com

www.zoemckey.com

Thank you for choosing my book! I would like to show my appreciation for the trust you gave me by giving a **FREE GIFT** for you!

Get it visiting www.zoemckey.com

The checklist talks about *5 key elements of building self-confidence* and contains extra actionable worksheets with practice exercises for deeper learning.

Learn how to:

- Solve 80% of you self-esteem issues with one simple change
- Keep your confidence permanent without falling back to self-doubt
- Not fall into the trap of promising words
- Overcome anxiety
- Be confident among other people

# Table of Contents

# Prologue: The Psychology of Procrastination

Maybe tomorrow. Today is tomorrow's yesterday.

Is this procrastination? Yes, because procrastination is a very highly motivated state. We are motivated to do nothing. We want to avoid any obstacle, problem or difficulty.

According to Donald Marquis, "Procrastination is the art of keeping up with yesterday".

Procrastination slows down all development. Crashes our Goals, and replaces action with anger and despair.

People who procrastinate tend to blame others for their failure and surging emotions. Their brain gets foggy; their spirit takes a dive. They no longer see their goals and give up their success voluntarily.

"Failure is simply the opportunity to begin again, this time, more intelligently." – Henry Ford

Many of us are afraid of failure, afraid to make a mistake. This feeling dominates our daily lives.

Every reason has to be taken seriously if it can hinder achieving your goals. There are beliefs stating procrastination is a normal human reaction.

I would call it a bad habit.

What is procrastination? Let's try a different approach.

A)  – to start something – if we don't start it, there is nothing to complete. (Yes! That's a relief. Really?)

B)  – to complete something – some tasks are ongoing.

Why do most people procrastinate? Because we are human?

What role do the following have in your procrastination?

- TV? Series filled with "deep thoughts" or talk shows? (And much more.)

- The Internet, where people spend hours opening their minds to a different form of brainwashing? Facebook, Twitter, and the other social networking sites don't put food on the table and don't provide our clothes – unless you are that one in a million user who does successful advertising on them. Everything has limits.

- Smartphones are useful; that's why we use them. Then become their slaves. Meaningless, empty conversations, texts, messages are serious obstacles in the liberation of ourselves.

Procrastination is the gravedigger of success. The difference between success and failure is Action. I mentioned this previously, and you will hear more about it in this book.

Procrastination is a highly motivated state. We are motivated to do nothing, to avoid difficulties, obstacles, and emotionally intolerable situations.

*"Motivation is what gets you started. Habit is what keeps you going."* Jim Rohn.

Keep in mind this very apt quote. By the end of the book, you will read some repeatedly occurring thoughts and statements. This is done to engrain them better.

Many times we know what to do, why to do it and how to do it. We just haven't gotten to that gripping and unpleasant situation and time that we absolutely must do it. Some people work this way. If there is no coercive force, they just sit and pass the time, which is actually their life.

Keeping the bad habit called Procrastination has a lot to do with our egos. We do everything we can to keep this habit. Often subconsciously. That's how someone can become unsuccessful. Procrastinating is a way of life for many of us. Often they reach for this tool because it is the easiest, the most convenient, and requires the least amount of effort. After a while, though...

When you have a goal or a task to do, after a while, you realize that you are just putting it off and putting it off. When you realize this, you should immediately start doing something else, something small. Do something that makes you happy, that you enjoy and raises your level of motivation. After that, you might find it easier to return to the basic task and take the steps leading up to solving the problem.

It is easier to have a continuous momentum than get up to speed, go full force, then come to a stop. Then full force again and relax. These ups and downs really zap your energy, your enthusiasm, and cloud your motivation.

If you are constantly in action, constantly making decisions, doing something, you enter the flow, and you will have the rise in your life you have dreamt of. It will be a lot easier to do anything. Trust me. Give it a try!

A few years ago there was a research group called Procrastination Group, with more than forty researchers studying the phenomena of procrastination. Amongst other things, they stated that there is a connection between age, gender, and procrastination.

Kids don't procrastinate. When they are hungry or thirsty, they let you know right away, quite forcefully. No waiting and procrastinating. They start crying – full power. They need a diaper change right now, not tomorrow or next month. Little ones work this way. This is how we used to work too.

Then we started learning habits from our surroundings. The majority of young people – college age or so, till they are about thirty as many people start their studies later – 70-75 percent are procrastinators. Out of older adults, only 25-30 percent of them are still in the trap of procrastination as they already experienced the downside of procrastination.

Women vs. men comparison are tilted for women. Women tend to procrastinate less than men because in their case life cycles can have a large influence.

What is the purpose of breaking a habit?

What is the negative you want to change from? Or is there a positive you would like to change to?

People, in general, don't dare to change because they think they have something to lose.

Anyone who falls into the pit of procrastinating, they can only do better. In school – I mean the traditional system of the academic institution - we got used to learning predefined answers and information to standard questions asked by teachers. Kids just spit out learned junk because they are not forced to learn about the world outside the walls. Everything is calculated and anticipated. A good grade just shows how cleverly and effectively a person can make himself or herself dependent on others. A future slave worker who is only able to work with directions from a superior.

Nowadays most people, including the so-called leaders, play on your emotions. Most often, fear and greed are motivating emotions. They feed most people's procrastinations. This book is for all those who are looking for a way out of the labyrinth of procrastination.

This book is intended for those who want and are willing to change.

*"My best friend is the one who brings out the best in me."* Henry Ford stated at a reception. His words are worth considering.

# Chapter 1: What Type Of Procrastinator Are You?

One thing is clear for everyone. The reason we don't dare to change is that we think we have something to lose.

The weak wait for the opportunity, the strong make it happen.

What type of person are you? Strong and decisive? Or someone who needs approval? Or someone who needs an audience? Do you need someone to cheer you on? To loudly praise your accomplishments? Or are you possibly one of those who can only blow their nose on command?

When we are awake, most of our actions are governed by our emotions... and that is the result of our thoughts.

Everything is decided in the head. Influenced by our Conscious or Subconscious, we do something and do it over and over and over again... or we just sit there, like in shock and wait for something to happen.

Studying the subject, relevant literature and habits of people, I came to the conclusion that the practitioners of the art of Procrastination can be divided into seven categories. Everyone has a dominant trait, and one or more of the less dominant traits can also be found.

1. **The Avoider Procrastinator** – It's all good. It will all work out somehow. It has never been that something didn't happen.

   No need to make a big deal out of it or blow it out of proportion. Live a little! They are the ones who go with the flow.

They lack sufficient motivation, so they do not make the first actual step. They are the people who give up their dreams for the benefit of others. They start working with a particular company because that's what their partner or boyfriend or girlfriend wants.

They get a degree because that's what their parents expect from them. They don't say no so they can avoid having to resist someone or something. They go with the flow and move only when the waves crash over their heads.

2. **The Perfectionist Procrastinator** – They won't start working on something unless all the conditions are met and they have all the information to do the work. They meticulously collect everything they think they need to solve the problem. They spare no time and effort on the preparations, safeguard themselves several times over (as much as they can) against unexpected failures. They overcomplicate their own situation and run out of

time, or they start over in a slightly different way or get lost in the details and lose sight of the Goal.

3.  **The Dreamer Procrastinator** – They can dream the most colorful of dreams. They can come up with more and more details. There is nothing that can limit their rambling imagination. They spend most of their time formulating their thoughts. You wouldn't want to miss an important detail. They can dream the task to be so beautiful and perfect; it would be a sin actually to implement it. They just keep coming with shiny new details.

    When it's time to take the actual step, that's when they say "We still have time! I want to think it all through so I have the big picture." That's how they delay the moment of doing what they've dreamt of.

4.  **The Negative Procrastinator** – Rejects any idea that is not his own right off the bat. When you present your own idea to him, he immediately begins to explain why it cannot be done. He finds

some fault in everything he needs to remedy and only then can he start, otherwise... He is the one always searching for the weak link till he finds one. There must be something that could cause a problem, and he cannot begin until he finds it. This attitude is typical of people who do things just to spite you.

5. **The Worrier Procrastinator** - But what if...? This type of person is afraid of his own shadow when it comes to doing something. Every little obstacle is a bottomless abyss or unscalable mountain. He torments and tortures himself till the waves crash over his head. Keeps whining about how much work he has. At the slightest resistance or adverse opinion/circumstance, he produces another catastrophe theory in his mind. Stops dead in his tracks and will not move until he is certain that it was just a false alarm. Then another wrench in the machine and everything starts all over again.

6. **The Panic Monger Procrastinator** -- He is the new and improved version of the Worrier

Procrastinator, with one difference. He has already started the work; he is going at it, driving his peers, without a plan. At the first sight of trouble, he panics. Starts looking for a scapegoat right away. *You, you and you, you are all to blame. Doesn't even occur to him to look for a solution to move on. I told you it was going to be all wrong... This is not the way to do it. It's just not a good idea. Timing was bad. We are running out of time. What are we going to do? We are going to get reprimanded. It is all your fault. You should all be doing something and none of you is doing anything.* Everyone is blamed for the crisis except him. He doesn't assume responsibility for what happened.

7. **The Overachiever Procrastinator** - He is the one who takes on everything without thinking. He will take care of it all, this is his job, even though it's not. He is the one who works a lot and takes on even more. Often he takes on other people's responsibilities, and things start to get chaotic. Thus the efficiency of his work is reduced, and he gets little done. He is the one who just goes and

goes without a vision, often without a plan. The space around them is not organized.

# Chapter 2: The Reasons of Procrastination

Uncertainty, fear of failure – which people experience as a threat –, the fact that people are unable to cope with certain things, the subconscious fear... these reasons are dependent on the person and situation.

Getting into the habit of procrastinating is a very complex and lengthy process. Each person has their own story on this matter, and everyone should develop their own strategies and tactics for dealing with it.

The following list presents the main reasons leading to procrastination. The first five are the most common; these are followed by less powerful reasons, lurking in the shadows. These round out the complete list to give you a more comprehensive image.

1.) **Being overworked**. Things start to pile up. You don't even remember which task is more important. When there is too much to do it is difficult to prioritize. In this case, in your desperation, you start working on the one with the closest deadline. "Urgent" and "important" lose significance. Sometimes you just do something because it is an easy fix. This way you can feel efficient and thus deceive yourself.

2.) **Boring work.** Doing something you do not enjoy and don't see a way out of it. There is no impossible situation, just laziness, sloth and similar excuses. There is a lot of human suffering, sorrow behind them. Maybe it would be a good idea to think and find the original meaning of what you are supposed to be doing. A task is monotonous if it is tiresome and makes you sleepy. Doing the same thing day after day gets boring if you cannot find something interesting in it, something that you like. People working at the same place for years most often can't find anything motivating.

3.) **Fear.** Two extremes of this feeling will lead to procrastination.

a) Fear of responsibility. When someone stops procrastinating, he comes face to face with uncharted areas of responsibility. That scares him, so he starts procrastinating again. Till he becomes an emotionally responsible adult he won't realize that he is responsible for his fate, he won't be successful and will keep procrastinating. Dare to take on the risk of error and failure. This is the only way he can learn and move towards the goal.

b) Fear of taking risks. This is a major barrier to personal development. Procrastinators see non-existing dangers in front of them. Their imagination exaggerates the risk. They need to realize that there is no action without risk. Without action there is no meaningful life, just vegetating and being lost in the maze of life. In time they realize that obstacles actually shows them the path to success.

4.) **Vanity**. Vain people are those who for example check their social media status often. They want to know how many likes their latest status or picture got on Facebook, Twitter or other social networking sites. They spend hours on the net surfing and reading enthusiastically about the life of the stars whom they want to resemble with.

5.) **Lack of motivation**. Why rush? It's good the way it is. Why should I kill myself with work? It will have to get done sooner or later, but for now, it can wait for a little. It's not like I get an award for it or anything. These people don't like to upset the status quo. Why rock the boat? Might get too stressed and get sick. This type of procrastinator, unless it is certain that he will be rewarded for action, prefers just to stay still, happy by being unnoticed, in the shadows.

6.) **Shame**. In this case, you feel that it is tough to ask for help. Shame is caused by pride, vanity or possibly laziness that prevent you from asking for help at the time of need and help you go on. Why should you bother others? You don't ask for help because you are ashamed of your assumed incompetence, and you don't want anybody to witness it.

7.) **Feeling paralyzed**. Why do you feel this way? Because the magnitude of the task is frightening. You need to change the attitude of Trying = Failure to Trying = Success. Take action, don't just hope for a miracle. Break down the problem into smaller steps, sub-steps and gradually execute them. These smaller and easier parts will get you moving again. Accept that it won't be perfect for the first time.

8.) **Inability to analyze**. Addendum to the previous point. You are unable to see through the task in detail. It's too big and too complicated. What are you supposed to do? What is it about? Which way should you be looking at it? You need to know what to do, but the most important thing is to know where to start.

9.) **The task is not clear**. In this case, it is not quite clear what is needed. Wrong or incorrect wording can lead to misunderstandings. Initial information amended with conflicting information can lead to unexpected results. You'd rather not deal with the issue and ask for more information than interfere with the status quo which is likely to create more disturbance.

10.) **Lack of priorities**. Those who do not list their tasks – in writing – according to importance and urgency tend to jump from task to task. Sometimes they just have to say no to things others want to pawn off on them. This will help them avoid being scattered. They usually postpone the first step because they are trying to get through the chaos around them. Be careful. If you lose sight of your goal, you could get into even bigger chaos.

11.) **Forgetfulness.** Many times you just get into the daily grind so deep that you forget the basic task. That's how the brain protects itself against breaking a routine. You tend to turn on the autopilot mode for the boring everyday life.

12.) **Nervousness.** We are afraid of personal confrontation, the potential unpleasant criticism or failure. The inner tension manifests itself this way in almost everybody's case. In this mindset, there is a greater risk of making a mistake, and one wants to avoid that... and procrastinates. Being nervous is often helpful because it mobilizes the reserves, which can us help get results.

13.) **Apathy**. Self-pity. Letting themselves down totally. These people feel that they need someone to control their fate because they are not able to decide anything for themselves. They neglect their duties and are mentally exhausted. They see the world as a foggy, dark place. Everything and everyone is against them. This diverts their attention, and they lose sight of their goal. Their own self-pity and self-blame crush them.

14.) **Dependence.** People rely on others because they feel they cannot do anything for themselves. They always need somebody's approval or guidance. Without external control they are like a ship without its captain, just drifting on the ocean without any direction.

15.) **Perfectionist.** These people obsessively strive for perfection. This can also be traced back to the fear of failure and fear of criticism. Often they tense up inside, muscles stiff, their brain gets foggy. They want to do their job without a mistake. They put the bar high. What would everyone say if they didn't do a perfect job? They cannot make a mistake! That would be a shame.

16.) **Taking advantage of others.** This person goofs off and slacks off till someone takes care of his work instead of him. He is in the background, pulling the strings till someone gets fed up and assumes a large portion of his task. It takes a lot of energy to be this manipulative, but he'd rather deal with that than the actual work. Actually, this is his method of operation. (This is one of the most damaging manifestations of procrastination.)

17.) **External forces**. Until our area of operation is limited by external factors, it will be hard to get rid of the pressure. We just react, not act. We keep running after success and cannot catch up with ourselves. It can be very depressing, and it also generates an internal pressure, which can make one procrastinate.

18.) **Fatigue**. The excuse of fatigue is one of the most self-reassuring methods. There is no human on earth who has not deferred something at least once referring to fatigue. The antidote for it is rest. Consider the task as a challenge even if it still seems uninteresting for the second or third attempt.

19.) **Over-commitment.** We take on more than we can handle. We want to play on many fields at once what leads to complete chaos. We take on so many burdens that we are crushed under the weight of it. It is hard to hold things together and figure out where to start.

20.) **Lack of self-control**. This person is not looking at anything or anybody, just goes full steam ahead. Let's do it, whatever it may be and whatever the price. Straining, snarling, not caring about anything. Then suddenly switching to passive. Low self-control and high impulsivity most often lead to procrastination.

21.) **Sickness.** Internal and external negative effects weaken the human body. It leads to getting sick which effectively postpones taking an action. The physical, emotional and psychological traumas strengthen the desire to procrastinate. The mind hits the bottom, the body's defense mechanism takes over.

Spending hours in front of the TV and computer is the nest of procrastination. The meaningless and empty programs, reports and information playing on your emotions and senses can cause the postponement of actual tasks.

# Chapter 3: The Consequences of Procrastination

Many of us do not see the destructive nature of procrastination. They just don't want to be disturbed by anyone. They just want their days to plod along nicely and easily... and they want to plod along with them.

This is not how life works. Some things need to be taken care of right away or today, maybe this week. Everyone has periodically repeating tasks with different regularity. Some tasks, jobs, and activities are ongoing.

That's why I need to talk about short-term procrastination and long-term procrastination.

There are quite a few jobs and tasks that fall into the group of short-term procrastination, like a project with a short deadline, a cell phone bill that must be paid by the 10th and so on. When the deadline is reached, the bad feeling and mood caused by procrastination is gone. So it's more tolerable after the deadline but in the meantime tension, a feeling of stress and discomfort are considerably high.

Who needs that?

Long-term procrastination is when someone procrastinates over something that has no specific deadline. For example, if you have to self-start a career – most often a venture – initially there is no deadline because nothing is happening until it is actually started. Other examples are family troubles, start to live a healthy lifestyle, getting in a relationship or breaking up with somebody. There is an infinite number of combinations for the possible situations and cases.

With no deadline, panic as a motivating factor rarely occurs. There is no trigger. There is nothing to remind you of the consequences of procrastination and possibly limit it. It just stretches and stretches till the end of time.

We tend to talk more about short-term procrastination because it can create much more spectacular and "fun" situations due to its specific deadlines.

Long-term procrastination produces hidden results rather than something outstanding or highly inefficient. This type of procrastination makes people outside observers, and at times they become outside observers in their own lives as well. They are frustrated because they have not even taken the first step to making their dreams happen, to achieve their goals.

In my opinion, there shouldn't be groups of procrastinators and non-procrastinators. We all do it, just not on the same level. Many people cannot live their lives without deadlines. There are those who live their whole life (almost) without a worry.

Don't beat yourself up about procrastinating. Do not judge. Just simply recognize the fact. You will have a bigger chance to act against it if you admit it – the sooner, the better –, you will waste less time. Don't think too much. Just do it!

There is a price for everything; intellectually and emotionally and - this is the most unpleasant for most of us - financially as well. Just pay it. It is not as bad as living unsuccessfully, in the shadows.

Procrastinating contrasts two crucial things, and there is a conflict about it in our subconscious:

- We all want something and
- We are all afraid of something.

The manifestation of these two things radically affects our lives.

Breaking the habit of procrastination or the battle against it starts with a decision. You must decide because it is up to you how you live your life.

OK. I will make a decision... Tomorrow. Maybe tomorrow. - You keep postponing that certain something till tomorrow.

*"Tomorrow is the busiest time of the year."* Spanish proverb.

If you cannot decide, you procrastinate. When you're forced to decide you feel cornered. This is a classic situation known in the animal kingdom, and you have two options:

- Rear up like a cornered bear and confront your lazy and procrastinating self, fight with all your might, kicking and screaming to get out of the tight spot, clawing and biting at the trap of procrastination and you escape. Or...


- Tuck your tail between your legs and find a deep, dark hole, resigned to the fact that that's it, you cannot do anything for yourself, let life put you in a cage and lead you on a leash. This means the loss of self-esteem. You blame the world, and a large part of your human relationships are left behind in the process.

Irritability, restlessness and messy human relationships. This short and concise sentence sums up the essence of this chapter.

Only your thoughts are your own. Everything that happens around you is largely independent of your will. Your thoughts affect your feelings, your inner world. Your emotions influence your actions, your achievements and your way of life.

If you think it's easy, it will be easy, if you think it's difficult, it will be difficult. Everything is decided in your mind.

We don't dare to change because we think we have something to lose.

What can we lose?

The answer to this question will always depend on the individual. Everybody is born with the ability to control their mind. Many are not even aware of this because they have not heard about it at home, and it is not taught in school. There are those who know about self-control but don't use it out of convenience and fail to take advantage of this talent. This is a form of procrastination as well.

They are losers, and it shows in their everyday lives as well. Plagued by sickness. Fear and worry poison their lives. Uncertainty and indecision keep them in their spot. As a direct consequence, frustration and discouragement will not let them out of poverty's grip. They are characterized by negative human qualities such as envy, anger, hatred and prejudice.

Am I able to remedy the mistakes of yesterday? Am I able to undo the pain I caused, take back spoken words? No. Yesterday is buried, and I won't think of it ever again.

This is now. This moment is the basis of what will happen in the future. Start the change. You tend to forget a crucial thing. The longer you delay, the more time of your precious life is wasted. There is a very important rule about using time. You only have twenty-four hours a day at your disposal and that's all there is. It doesn't matter who you are, how much money and power you have, you won't have more than twenty-four hours a day.

Time cannot be provisioned, and cannot be stored. It will pass and be gone. It's up to you and you only how you use your time. You have twenty-four hours in your day, Bill Gates has twenty-four hours in his day, and even Abraham Lincoln had twenty-four hours a day at his disposal. That's the point, to take advantage of your time rations.

# Chapter 4: The Method of Overcoming Procrastination

In the process of discovering a law of nature, psychologists came up with a golden truth. The mind is capable of achieving anything you believe in. I'm not talking about education, degrees or academics.

Napoleon Hill was among the first who stated in a comprehensible form this fundamental law, which allows all of us to achieve our goals. He stated the following: "Whatever the mind of man can conceive and believe, it can achieve."

A concrete example is Thomas Edison, one of the world's greatest inventors. He only went to school for three months – school as we know it, an institution providing formal academic studies – and yet his discoveries are still positively affecting the entire human civilization.

Regardless of how many times in the past you've failed or what your goals and hopes are, you decide your own fate and set your own goals.

There is a powerful force with no limits, and it is completely under your control. This force is greater than poverty and lack of education. This force is greater than the sum of all your fears and prejudices. With this force, you can take control over your own mind. You can guide it anywhere to achieve anything you want.

You have absolute power over your thoughts!

When you talk about delaying the start or the deficiencies of your working conditions or even just think about them, you direct your mind to attract these adverse conditions.

Whatever you nurture your mind with, you will attract to yourself.

Everyone is born with the ability to control their mind. Anyone can control their mind and put it in their service. Those who learn this are the winners of life. They are the ones who actually use what they get:

- Health
- Inner peace
- Ability to make decisions
- Freedom from fear and anxiety
- Positive attitude
- A certain quality and quantity of financial security.

You must know what you want and be aware of the impact procrastination has on your life. Procrastination is your biggest enemy, and you are feeding it – especially with being passive. Let's look at the steps you should consider.

a) The first and most important step is to admit being a procrastinator and deciding to break the habit. Make this your goal. This is your first task. This could be your life goal as well. If you can determine what you want to accomplish in your life, write it down and visualize it.

b)  Learn all about procrastination – what are the causes and what you can do about it. (The previous and following chapters talk about this.)

c)  Develop a strategy and action plan: build a list of the tasks, which you can start without procrastination. The following chapters will show you the steps, focusing on the different types of procrastination.

d)  Carry out your plan. This will be the biggest challenge you are going to do successfully.

Change your habits. After all, this is the surest way to overcome procrastination. It is a bad habit you learned throughout your life.

Procrastination started out as some defense mechanism. We wanted to push the boundaries of childhood further and wanted to live in a carefree era. So we started to learn the habit of procrastination (subconsciously) as we were growing up.

Growing up we experienced some changes in the attitude of others towards us. We were not the cute little spoiled girls or boys anymore. They started to impose demands on us. We were given tasks that were barely explained. Do this, do that. Adults didn't overlook our mischievousness. As an answer, we started defying them by not doing what they asked on purpose.

Procrastination born in defiance turned into a habit. We developed all those bad habits that hold us in place that are resistant to any change within our comfort zone. They destroy the smallest notion of change.

You must take action against these habits. Adapt a habit of fighting against bad habits. That's what you are doing right now. If you have reached this point in the book, you are on your way to get rid of one of the worst habits of people, procrastination.

You have to apply what you will learn here yourself. It is never too late to have a happy childhood, but your second childhood depends on you and no one else. When you have to struggle with yourself for what you really desire, don't ever give up. It is up to you to quit procrastinating and have order in your life.

Learning the habit of doing everything at the right time is a serious challenge.

Only today matters.

Today is the day when you take the first, very important step in the creation of the new you. Just think how many people were making plans for today yesterday and today they are no longer among us.

You are a lucky man because today is a gift from your life. Earn it. Show that you deserve it. You have another chance to become the person who is there inside you. Free yourself. Be purposeful.

Forget yesterday. Do no waste your time on the misfortune of yesterday, lamenting the failures. Can anyone undo harmful spoken words and pain caused? No. Yesterday is gone.

Every hour of today is invaluable. Make it priceless. You are not wasting time. Action eliminates procrastination. Take action and thus prove to yourself that you are important. Your loved ones are important because you are no longer a slacker and a procrastinator. (You don't steal food, clothes, and security from your loved ones.) Procrastination means all this, in case you were not aware.

Analyze the tasks. Get a notepad just for this purpose.

Write your main goal that you would like to achieve in your life on the first page. Determine the circumstance, situation or action that you can accept as your idea of success. Remind yourself that only your mind can limit your goals... or others' negative influence if you let that happen and infect your mind.

On the other side write down, clearly defined, what you offer to life in exchange for achieving your goals.

Write down where you stand at the moment to start giving your offerings. Something for something. It is very important. Memorize them. What you want to achieve and what you are willing to give in return? Repeat them daily, at least ten times.

On a new sheet of paper write down ten tasks, you will do today. You have to do the same daily for 28 days. I am asking you to pick ten different tasks to do every day.

You will have ten new tasks to complete every day. They cannot be repeated or postponed to the next day.

1.) Pick a task of the ten tasks for the day. One you have been postponing the longest and is the most pressing.

2.) List the reasons for completion of the selected task.

3.) List the excuses why you have not started it.

4.) Compare the lists from point 2.) and 3.). What do you think about seeing next to each other the pressing reasons for completion and the excuses for delaying?

5.) Start working on the selected task. Break the process down into smaller parts.

6.) Once you finish, start with the second task. Don't put it off. Do not postpone.

Twenty-eight days later you will have 280 identified tasks, out of that you completed at least twenty-eight. Write your daily plans down the night before and read through them in the morning. Clarify them if necessary.

# Chapter 5: Strategies for Surviving and Overcoming Procrastination

How should you break the habit of procrastination?

There is no better time to fight procrastination than right now. This is the moment!

In this chapter, you will find practical advice for strategies on how to overcome procrastination.

I will talk about the tactical steps separately in the following chapters when I present the seven basic types of procrastinators. You are one of the seven types. I am one of them, too.

Do not jump in until you have decided that you will do your part without hesitation. You need to do your part to make it happen. Take 28 days of your life, the next 28 days. It is very important.

*"Act as if it were impossible to fail."* I found this idea by Dorothea Brande in an old notebook of mine, framed in red. If you get stuck, and you have to skip a day for a reason, you will have to start over from day one. Only a completely flawless and continuous 28 days will be productive. No matter for what reason/reasons you stop — you are flooded with negative thoughts or you are buried at work or go on vacation or get married — you still have to go back to day one. Do it for yourself and do it perfectly. Day after day. Do it.

Nothing is mandatory. It is all up to you. You made the particular decision that will take you out of your comfort zone. I am not selling a pig in a poke. You are doing this for your own good.

The most effective antidote for procrastination is an activity requiring discipline.

What does this mean to put it more simply? What is discipline in this context?

Discipline equals doing something even when you don't want to do it.

That's right. Because procrastination reduces your effectiveness. It holds you back, and it is an obstacle in your path to success. This is true both in private life and at work, either professionally or in any other part of life.

Open the aforementioned notepad on a new page. The first step is to:

a) Write a to-do list. Write down absolutely everything you need to do the next day. Then prioritize the by marking the most burning ones URGENT. Most people only by doing the urgent things during the day become dead tired by evening. This is the method of putting out fires, or catching up in other words. It should not be used long term though because it is exhausting. Here is the antidote:

- Write down your to-do list for the next week or month or possibly year creating not urgent but important groups. One of the biggest problems is that as long as something is not urgent, we just keep postponing it. When we get to a point that something becomes urgent, we can no longer procrastinate, but we create a very stressful and unhealthy atmosphere for ourselves.

- I suggest you concentrate on the important groups, do every important task at its right time and save yourself some nerves

b)  Write a not to do list. Write down anything you don't want to do or does not need to be done. For example:

-   Do not waste your time in front of the television with watching/listening shows or materials that are not useful or you cannot learn from them. They won't help you in anything.

-   You do not need to meet people who just waste your time with their meaningless conversations.

c)  Divide the larger tasks into smaller parts. To the classic question "How do you eat an elephant?" there is the classic answer "Bite per bite".

For example: how do you write a book? Xxx Then you start thinking and divide the whole thing into smaller steps. Like this:

- **Task 1** – Figure out what you want to write about. Select a topic.
- **Task 2** – Summarize the book in one sentence.
- **Task 3** – Start collecting material on the chosen topic. Explore how other people feel about the matter. Read books, watch videos, listen to podcasts on the topic, talk to strangers and take notes.
- **Task 4** – Start outlining and writing the book.
- **Task 5** – Publish the material in printed form or audiobook.
- **Task 6** – Promote your product.

It is good to work with smaller parts because when one part is finished, you can finally cry out "Yeah, it's done!" and move on to the next step. It is a liberating feeling.

Most tasks take more than an hour, and they can be quite time-consuming. Sometimes they can take weeks, months or even longer. If this is the case divide them into more sub-tasks up to the point, they become manageable.

d)  The technique of positive statements is about powerful questions (this is known as Einstein's mother effect).  What is a good and powerful question look like? Why do we care about the answer? Now that's an excellent and powerful question.

Our brain works with questions. Ask yourself tough, positive questions to make your brain work on the answers. Your subconscious is the most effective partner assisting you in the battle against procrastination. To highlight the importance of powerful questions, it needs some explanation.

Ever since we were little kids, our brains worked with questions, not with statements. Why is the ice cold? Why is it dark at night? Why is the grass green? These are the questions of a small child. Kids don't make statements like the ice is cold. The night is dark. The grass is green. We grew up asking. By asking we broadened our knowledge, our experience, and our emotions, too.

e) Start with what you don't like but needs to be done. It is better to be done with unpleasant things first, it's a relief. The rest seems easy afterward.

f) Pay the price of what you want to do or what you want to become. Think about your previous difficulties and you realize it is not as difficult to pay the price of your dream, as it is to continue living without success.

g)   Reward yourself. Every time you check something off your to-do list – a task completed or a section finished – reward yourself. Something that feels good and makes you happy. It is important to keep in mind the financial term "pay yourself first" principle. Some aspect of this has got to motivate you.

Now write down all the things you have wanted to do and so far only postponed.

## Chapter 6: How to Break the Habit of Procrastination?

Do the first step right now. Decide that from now on you will replace procrastination as a habit with a different habit. This will be the *"I will do it right now"* habit. (Or name it whatever you feel is best for you.)

Procrastination is a bad habit - you are going to replace with a better habit. You decided that you will love yourself and love this day - today. This is the happiest day of your life because you have started on the road to success. Success can be anything. You choose the goal of your dreams. Visualize it and impose a deadline for reaching it. Think about it, imagine the process and write it down step by step.

The best way to do this is to get a piece of paper and write down the 10 most important goals you have been dreaming of since you were a child.

Commit yourself to reaching them!

It seems immature, but believe me, it is very important and it works. People usually have two reasons they don't want actually to write down what they want.

1. They are afraid if they write it down someone – mostly themselves – will make them accountable for it.
2. In reality, they have no concrete plans, no life goals.

Write down ten of your most important goals. Rank them in order of importance. Ranking them is very important. Have a system of criteria. As simple as possible, max. three to five parameters. Rate each parameter from 1 to 10.

For example:

1. What is your main goal? (Mark the ranking from 1 to 10. Caution! When you are doing the ranking, first place is worth 10 points, second place is worth 9 points and so on, down to the last place with only one point in value.)

2. How important is it for you to achieve this goal? (1-10)

3. How would it impact you if you didn't reach this goal? (1-10)

I gave you three parameters that you can use. I suggest adding at least two of your own to refine your quantifiable rankings. Using only the first three parameters often brings out a tie among your goals' importance. (The fourth parameter could be „How urgent is this?" but this is the "putting out fires" method, don't use it long term, it could affect your efficiency! Use your brain. Find parameters that bring relevant results. Apply the powerful question technique.)

In case there is a tie, you should have one more criteria in your reserves (or you need to come up with a new one) that will help you in your decision. This will require painstaking work, but you are going to do everything in the wake of your decision to be able to move on.

Within a few days you will start using more and more parameters, almost unnoticed. This is a step up for you, your progress in the fight against procrastination. I suggest using up to ten parameters as processing too many aspects is time-consuming and might come at the expense of efficiency. This does not mean that you should stop looking for new ones. The more parameters you discover and write down the more accurate your result can be. However don't use more than ten parameters for determining a goal.

Always use the most appropriate ones. You will get the best results using seven parameters. I say this from experience.

Approach your list both from a mental and emotional side. Ask yourself and have sound reasoning as to why your goals are in the positions where they are.

How do you rate your own survey?

We talked about the To Do list in the previous chapter and important and urgent items.
All your goals written on your list are important to you. Depending on the result there should be:

1. Very important – the average of parameters should be 8 or greater (8<X)

2. Important - the average of parameters should be between 6 and 8 (6<X<8)

3. Can wait (important, but not urgent) – the average of parameters is under 6 (X<6)

X means the average value of the result here.

Specific examples:

1) Working with 3 parameters. a=10 b=9 c=9

   X=a+b+c=10+9+9=28/3=9.33. Thus X=9.33.

   8<X=9.33. So this is a very important goal.

2) Working with 5 parameters, because we have a tie between two particular goals after using the first 3 parameters. (See previous example.)

   a=10 b=9 c=9 d=5 e=4

   X=a+b+c+d+e=10+9+9+5+4=37/5=7.4

   Thus X=7.4.

   6<7.4<8. This goal is "only" important.

Be *honest and objective*. These are two magic words to keep in mind. Listen to their content and meaning and use your brain based on them.

# Chapter 7: The Avoider Procrastinator

The Avoider Procrastinator is the one who does not take any actual step to change the situation due to lack of proper motivation. He is among those who give up their dreams for the benefit of others. He gets enrolled in college or starts a training course because his parents or his partner expect that.

They don't say no so they can avoid having to resist someone, perhaps a situation or condition. He has a job he doesn't like, that he doesn't find any pleasure in.

He doesn't see a way out of his situation and simply goes with the flow. When the waves crash over his head, he will move just to be able to stay afloat.

The Avoider Procrastinators rely on others for choosing a direction or making a decision. They are not independent. They feel they are not able to do anything for themselves. They always need agreement, approval, and guidance. Without external advice they are like a ship without its captain, drifting on the ocean of life without a purpose.

Many times they get paralyzed under the weight of all the accumulated tasks, unable to see through each task in detail.

*Too much and too complicated.* Many times he doesn't know what he should be doing.

*What is this about? How should I approach this particular thing?*

The most important thing is to figure out where to start. When the task is not clear enough, he immediately comes to a halt. Bad or confusing wording can lead to errors, and he just wants to avoid that. He'd rather wait a little longer in getting started and rather not deal with obtaining more information and threaten the status of sweet idleness.

So far I've listed what kinds of features identify the Avoider Procrastinator. These features are all bad habits.

Let's look at the most efficient method to replace these habits.

Write down on a blank sheet of paper: **This is the only day for me!**

What does this mean exactly?

- Write down at least ten things you must do today. This list can include things like calling your parents, washing the car or going to the hair stylist.

- Then rank them and group them depending on whether they can be resolved from home or you actually need to leave. Prioritize within the group. What can you take care of on the phone, email or any other form without having to exit the house? Leave only when you must.

- Impose a deadline to get them done. It can be thirty minutes or 2 hours. You can determine the time frame for the fixed tasks, and then you can take care of the rest based on a preplanned route. Be effective!

Be ready not to succeed the first time. No big deal. You can give it another try.

On the first day getting 50% is an excellent result.

**Caution**! This is only the first day. You will have to do the same thing every day, for 28 consecutive days. Every day you will have to write ten new things on your To Do list.

Do not repeat them. This way you will take care of the long delayed, almost forgotten things still waiting to be resolved. You will step out of your comfortable routine. You will leave your comfort zone and start creating solutions.

When you are done, be thankful that you could do them. Be grateful.

Be grateful for the fact that the remaining hours of today represent eternity.

Be grateful for being lucky as these hours are priceless gifts.

Be thankful for being able to reach your goals. This is a great advantage over those who thanked yesterday for their lives and today are no longer among us.

You have the possibility to become the person you want to be.

You only have one life and think of it as a unit of time. Think about your life. If you are wasting your time with procrastinating, you destroy your own life. Maximize the use of every hour of the day because you realize you cannot get these hours back. You cannot put them in a bank account, thinking you will use them one day. A dying man would give all his money to breath.

How do you value the hours you have? Make them priceless!

Take care of today's tasks today! From now on you do not know the taste of defeat! You are unrivaled in the world!

As the days go by, you will be more effective and get more done. After two weeks you should only miss a task in exceptional cases.

This is very important! After each completed task checked off, reward yourself. What should the reward be? That's totally up to you. As you progress, raise the bar higher and higher, helping yourself along.

Learn to see the joy in things. Remember, you are as happy as you want to be.

# Chapter 8: The Perfectionist Procrastinator

The Perfectionist Procrastinators think that only a perfectly done job is a good job. They won't start working on something or implementing a task unless all the conditions are met and they have all the information needed to do the work. They document even the smallest details and collect everything they think they may need to complete the task.

They obsessively strive for perfection. This can be traced back to the fear of failure and criticism. Often they tense up inside, muscles stiff, their brains get foggy. They want to do their job without a mistake. They put the bar high. *What would everyone say if they didn't do a perfect job?* They cannot make a mistake that would be a shame. Their dissatisfaction with themselves indicates a lack of self-confidence. They spend a ton of time and effort on preparations and safeguard themselves several times over against unexpected situations.

Most often they overcomplicate themselves and things. With that, the chance of running out of time increases. Their ego is so big that wouldn't notice help offered by others.

Perfectionist Procrastinators check their email often. They are curious how many likes they are getting on Facebook, Twitter or other social networking sites.

They get so lost in the details that they lose sight of their goal.

If you recognize yourself, you have an important decision to make. You will win the battle against the bad habit of procrastination by replacing it with a pragmatic and realistic new habit. Promise yourself that to succeed you will do as described below **for the next 28 days**, day after day. Take me as your mentor and act for yourself to break from the trap you've set.

On a clean sheet of paper write down ten things needing to be done, which you have been postponing for a long time because of the above reasons. Only ten. After writing them down, rank them in order of importance or urgency.

Think about them and impose a deadline, in space and time. The deadline should be realistic. You should define it so no matter what happens you will do your tasks by the specified time. (Specify it by day and time.) So that there will be a list of tasks to do, ranked by importance or urgency with their deadlines.

There are some critical questions you should think through in regards to what lays ahead of you. Take your tasks one at a time – all ten – and examine each the following way:

a) Do I have all the necessary information to do the job? (Y/N)

b) Can I get the missing data/information to carry out the task before the deadline? (Y/N)

c)  Am I able to finish the job as required by the
    deadline? (Y/N)

These questions are intended as a guide. You can write more questions if they help. They should be yes or no questions. Be careful not to ask the same thing, only with different words.

For every task have at least three targeted yes or no questions. If the answer is No to even one question, do not deal with that task. You would just waste your time with it, as you would not be able to complete it 100%.

Take another step, onto a new task. Do this day after day, each consecutive day - for 28 days. Every day write ten new tasks on your list, making sure that they are all different. After the first week, it will be easier to perform the above described.

**Caution**! We have a tendency to become arrogant. When you answer your questions and start selecting tasks, and there is little substantive work left, you feel like you should write another list. Because you already know everything, and there is nothing new under the sun. That is when you are trapped in your routine.

In this case, take a look at your questions you answered No to and try a different point of view, ask another question which was not among the ones used in the first round. That's how you train your mind and subconscious so later on you will find the right direction more quickly.

For this method to be effective forming your new habit – I say it again – make a list.

Day after day.

This is what self-discipline means, which is one of the best qualities to fight procrastination.

# Chapter 9: The Dreamer Procrastinator

The Dreamer Procrastinator spends most of his day in autopilot mode. Often she is so immersed in her work that the actual job gets lost in the background. Sometimes she even forgets why she actually started what she is doing.

They can dream interesting and very colorful dreams. They expand them more and more, supplement these dreams with additional details. There is nothing to limit their vivid imagination. They spend most of their time formulating their thoughts.

They can dream the job to be so beautiful and perfect; but it would be a disaster to implement it.

When they can no longer put off the first step, then comes *"We still have time! I want to think it all through to have the big picture!"*

That's how they delay the moment of doing what they have dreamt of.

Another subspecies of Dreamer Procrastinators are those who know what they want, they can make good plans, but at the moment of practical implementation, their whole system comes to a halt. They stop and postpone a certain job till tomorrow or to a vague "later". They become depressed, their mood darkens. If they could, they would ask others to carry out the changes for them to avoid having to take responsibility. Sometimes someone does take their place, but they don't like that either as it hurts their pride.

They are standing still, waiting, suffering until they can't take it or till life hands them an alternative. Up until that moment they are getting more frustrated and unhappy. They cunningly try to avoid making a decision, even though that's what they need the most.

Meanwhile, the clock is ticking, life has its time limits. It would be helpful to learn to pay attention to these signals. By depending on them, you can change directions on time. Suffering means that you need to change something.

Are you happy and content? Continue the path and direction you are on. Yes, it's that simple. With a little self-confidence and initiative, you can make the life; you have dreamt of become reality. This is one factor that makes us human.

We have long risen from the level of instincts to the level of emotional – mental existence. Now we have to learn how we can live and interact with ourselves and with our environment.

If we are accepting of ourselves, then we don't have particular problems with our environment either. This means the ability to explore our emotions and motivations objectively.

We need to get back to reality and learn how to feel secure again.

Learn to love again. Love the real you, not the idealized dream version. Then you need to get to love the obstacles, because they show you what you can do when you succeed. You will be stronger.

Pay attention to the signals from your environment. Everything around you is alive. We are part of it all. The possibilities are in you; you just need to learn to take advantage of them. There is no use in having a talent, skills, or knowledge if you do not know how to use them.

Every day try a little harder than the day before. Every day add a little more to your previous list (and do it.)

Walk the path you have chosen. Many start out on the same path, then stop and give up before the finish. Many lose their faith, their confidence, or their endurance on the winding road. Say it out loud: **I will keep going**. Maybe success is waiting for you just beyond the next turn, at the finish line. It is also possible that you will have to take a lot of turns till you get to the finish. Hang in there and go all the way.

You cannot overcome procrastination by merely talking about it.

Take a new sheet of paper and write down all the things, tasks you have been delaying for the reasons mentioned.

Make a list of ten different tasks every day, for 28 days. One task cannot be on two lists. Quit dreaming, and apply yourself, with full force.

Number them by importance: first the most important, then the runner-up, the third and so on.

It seems like it's very meticulous and painstaking work. There is a meaning behind it. It will get rid of one of your worst habits engrained over the years. You are going to replace procrastination with a mentality related to a system. This is part of a new attitude regarding life.

1. Pick a task from your list, one you have been long delaying.

2. List the reasons for completion.

3. List the reasons why you haven't started it.

4. Compare the two lists. If a reason has a pro and con, neutralize them against each other. This leaves only the single yes or no reasons.

5. Leave only the strong reasons, cross out the rest with red. Keep considering the reasons and cross them out till only one remains.

If the reason is for completing the task, start immediately. If it is not deemed necessary, then don't worry about it.

# Chapter 10: The Negative Procrastinator

We were born to find our place in the world.

Many are waiting for the world to show them their place and show them where to go. It is a way of life too - if that's how you want to live.

When things don't turn out the way you wanted them to, or don't go your way, or you don't get tasks that resolve themselves, or they don't have an easy solution, that can certainly be a problem. Suddenly, everything becomes dark. You see rejection and resistance everywhere.

Either something is the way you want it or it shouldn't exist at all. *I won't do it...now. It's not the right time, or right method or the right people.*

Most people do things the way they first learned them and repeated them almost automatically their whole life. Daily activities become routine, then habit.

They get boxed in, and if they come across an unusual or unfamiliar situation, they will come to a stop. If things are not going according to the norm, they have a problem. What to do?

Everything is decided in the mind. Why do we say no? Why do we resist? What are the results of feeding our ego? What are the remote consequences of our negativity?

For example, if we don't do our job on time, it becomes worthless. If there is no value in our work, there is no reason to get paid for it. If we don't get paid, we can't pay our bills, buy food or clothes for our family and ourselves. We steal the possibility of a safe and peaceful life from our loved ones.

Is that what you want?

Of course not. Do something about getting rid of your bad habit of procrastination.

As long as people are in their comfort zones, it is hard to see the whole picture. Step out of the comfort zone.

Every time you find negative thoughts popping up, immediately replace them with their positive counterparts, and write them down on a new page in that particular notebook you started for your success in the fight against procrastination.

Make up your mind and make a decision: *From this moment on I'm only interested in why I should do a certain thing or what the reason to fulfill a task completely is.*

Every night write your To Do list for the next day. Include everything you need to accomplish that day. You should even list getting your prescription from the pharmacy or taking your spouse to the dentist.

In the morning, after you get up, read through your list again and make a note next to each of them why it is important to get it done. List the reasons for why it needs to get done. You teach your brain to think a certain way with the help of visualization. You can think of it as childish, but it is effective. If you did this on your own, you would not have to read this book.

Complete your list from the previous night with answers to the question "Why should I do it?"

Then start doing the tasks listed. **Caution!** Write down at least ten things (even if you have to squeeze your brain because you only have eight, there has got to be five things in your home needing to be done). You can only leave a quarter of it for the next day.

Be honest with yourself and do not cheat.

It is not going to be easy because you must defeat yourself. Yes, you must act against yourself. Do it, because that's the only way to change in the right direction.

The situation we are living in is a reflection of the process taking place in us. We recreate what's happening inside us in our surroundings as well. After the fifth or sixth day (possibly after the tenth for the slower-moving among us) the effects of the new method start to become perceptible. Your system starts to appear in your everyday life, and you can extend it to your environment as well. Because it is important for you.

By changing your attitude, you can change the course of events. You can create new paths and opportunities. First of all, *learn to love yourself*. Carefully look at everything, study things before you let them enter your mind, your soul, and your heart.

Don't let mean thoughts and despair enter your mind. Use your brain (read and educate yourself) and wisdom (learn from others as well).

Don't let your soul become arrogant.

Here are some previous thoughts from a different perspective.

1. Think about your life so far and learn to see yourself as a part of a whole.

2. Look ahead and educate yourself. Learning helps. Learn something new every day, something you didn't know or haven't done. Then practice what you've learned. Apply it.

3. Use your brain. You can count only on yourself.

4.  Be brave and take the initiative. Dare to take on new and so far unknown tasks. Regularly do things requiring effort and imagination.

5.  Do not leave things unfinished. It is up to you how much you reduce the pressure on yourself. Perform your tasks.

6.  Are you practical? If not, you can improve your skills. Paint and tinker. Create. Look around in your home and see what needs to be fixed and fix it. This is how you will be able to solve problems, which you have lacked the confidence to do before.

7.  Involve your senses. Make them work. Have a goal and complete it in theory, in thought. Then do it. Break that certain task into smaller parts and do it. Feel the joy in doing it. See the results.

The 28 days you are dedicating to do this, is only a fraction of what led you so far.

Consider what you need to do and what results you want to achieve. Put the rest of your life in first place and your values will change.

# Chapter 11: The Worrier Procrastinator

*Oh, what happens if...? Really... What's going to happen? When will we do it?*

The Worrier Procrastinator gets terrified of his own shadow when it's time to get started. He sees the smallest hole in his path as a bottomless abyss. The slightest resistance or push back scares him. He torments and tortures himself postpones his tasks till the waves crash over his head.

He keeps whining about the unfairness of life and how busy he is. There are a lot of things to take care of, and he is afraid of making a mistake or being unable to finish his job.

He stops at the first negative opinion or circumstance and will not move until he manages to calm down, convincing himself that it was just a false alarm. And that takes a lot of time. Then another small cloud comes and covers his sunshine and worrying starts over again.

Measure your abilities and limitations. Know your feelings and try to understand the reason for them. Rephrase your values so that they work for you and not against you.

*"Everything you want is on the other side of fear."* - Jack Canfield

This is one of the main reasons for procrastination. Face your fears!

Accept that they exist. Get to know your fears and it will be much easier to live with them. This is also a way to move on.

Once you start to understand the fear of responsibility and fear of risk, it will be easier to manage these feelings. Everything depends on your point of view and also on your attitude. This reminds me of a joke I once heard during a break at a training seminar:

There was this businessperson who, as the years passed and he was getting old, thought about death more and more. He reached a respectable age, died and found himself in front of St. Peter. The gatekeeper of Heaven warmly welcomed the businessperson.

- Mr. Rich! Towards the end of your life you have donated a lot to benefit the poor and the orphans, and because of this, you are allowed to choose. Where do you want to be for the resurrection? Heaven or Hell?

- In my earthly life, I was a businessperson, and I wouldn't make a decision before having all the necessary information. I would like to visit both places, if possible, and then choose. – Said Mr. Rich.

- No problem. Where should we start? – Asked St. Peter.

- Let's check out Hell first. – Answered Mr. Rich. They enter the gates of Hell and see some old, bald, portly gentlemen with blonde, brunette and redheaded vixens in their lap sitting on couches in shady groves, eating, drinking and chatting. That's how they wait for their judgment day.

- Hm, interesting. Let's see what Heaven is like. – Commented Mr. Rich. They go up to Heaven and what do they see? Some elderly, bald, portly gentlemen with blonde, brunette, redheaded vixens on their lap, sitting on couches in shady groves, eating, drinking and chatting. That's how they wait for their judgment day also.

- I don't understand. What is going on? I saw the same thing in Hell. – Marveled Mr. Rich.

- You are mistaken, sir! You saw carnal, pleasure-seeking women serving out their punishment in Hell, while in Heaven you saw men who lived exemplary lives on earth enjoying their well-deserved reward.

Why did I mention this joke? Because you never know if the reason for your fear is real or it only exists in your mind. All is a matter of perspective.

Experiencing fear in all aspects of life is natural. These emotions are present in all of us. Your attitude towards fear can be twofold:

A. You can overcome your fears. You can use them as tools to be stronger, to reach your goals.

B. You can let your fears gain control of you and hold you back from making your dreams come true.

You are holding this book because you already made the decision. You will overcome your fears and give up procrastination!

Find a task where others have failed. Learning from their failures you will succeed.

So...face your fears. If you do and follow these steps, you can find your greatest strength.

1. Ask yourself: What is the worst thing that can happen to me?

2. Write down the process and implications of this worst-case scenario as precisely as you can.

3. Prepare yourself mentally to accept it.

4. Write down every conceivable solution to avoid the worst.

5. Choose the solution you think is the best.

6. Start working on the task. Just do it, finish it.

7. By the guidelines of the previous six points, go to the next task.

On a clean sheet of paper in your notebook titled Overcoming Procrastination, make a list containing all those things – at least ten - you have been postponing because of your fears. Write the list in black or blue.

Then using a red pen write next to each task at least three reasons keeping you from carrying them out. For every "Fear Reason", written in red, write with green what you would do to abolish this particular Fear Reason.

It gives the most visible results if you create a spreadsheet, using columns, listing what is described above. The colors should make your list quite transparent. You should do this for 28 days, day after day.

Caution! Do this for 28 consecutive days. If for some reason — objective or subjective — continuity is interrupted, you will have to restart the 28 days with new tasks.

One task cannot be on two lists. Use your brain and shift it into active mode. Use your memory and find tasks to complete what you have been neglecting or postponing because of your fears.

There will be a minimum of 560 things you solve in your life during the days of action. Sounds good, right? If these occur again, you will have the solution ready.

# Chapter 12: The Panic Monger Procrastinator

A lot depends on you only. Are you able to do certain things or not? Of course, you are, and you should be proud of yourself.

See yourself as a winner. Your life is actually just about you. Every once in a while give yourself a pep talk about how great you are at certain things.

Make yourself a motivational album. Put everything in it that improves your mood. Everything has an opposite. We can only appreciate the light because of darkness. Cold days are followed by a warm season.

You are your own best friend and often your own worst enemy. Use your brain. Remember your childhood. Go back to your past in your mind as far as your memory lets you. What happened when you completed a particular thing or solved a problem? You were praised and maybe even rewarded. The more often you did the same task, the easier it became. You performed faster and better.

New challenges came. If you got a good grade in school, the sun was shining. If you didn't do well, or the grades were bad, you were punished. You have to earn your keep at work too, and many factors can pull the rug from under your feet.

All things come to an end. This short phrase often helped me through difficult moments, hopeless situations.

Take another sheet of paper for this chapter and divide it into four parts one under the other. Write down the following:

A. A reed – It is strong, thin and flexible.

B. An oak tree – It has been withstanding the storm of time for centuries. Its expansive roots go deep into the ground and its canopy offers protection and shelter to many creatures.

C. A sequoia pine – It has lived through and experienced a lot of things in the past thousand years. The storm of life cannot damage it. It bursts directly and majestically into the sky.

D. A big mountain – Its peaks are lost in the clouds. Only God has power over it.

Depending on the situation, you are the reed, the oak tree, the sequoia and the mountain. Visualize yourself. Depending on what needs to be resolved – along with the impeding factor – imagine yourself one of the things described above.

"Failure should be our teacher, not our undertaker. Failure is a delay, not defeat. It is a temporary detour, not dead end." - Denis Waitley

You have just started on a new path that leads you to the light and well-being. You feel like a new you.

"There are two things a person should never be angry at; what they can help, and what they cannot." - Plato

Life is not as complicated as we think it is. Let's clarify our thinking.

Keep calm.

On a new page in your notebook write in all caps: PANIC IS THE OPPOSITE OF CALM. I AM CALM.

To be able to deal with your goals clearly, you need to see with crystal clarity.

Write down all the things that need to be addressed. The list should have at least ten items that you have been postponing. Do this for 28 consecutive days.

Attention! Tasks on the list cannot be repeated. Your list must contain at least ten different items every day.

A. Vision

B. Goals

C. Action

You will have to find answers to these individual parts in each case. An action that is taken out of the context of vision and goals is not effective.

If you do the following in writing and while calm, you have started in the right direction. As the days go by you will find out if the right path was chosen or not.

Do not lose sight of the reason you are reading this book. You want to beat procrastination.

I would like to show you an example you could use in case you are a business owner; an employee or you simply want to change your life.

I will ask a lot of questions, and you will have to give honest answers.

1. **Vision**

   - What do you expect from your business?

   - How will your company look when it's viable? (The size you envisioned, as this will help you project your company's vision.)

   - Visualize the result, as you want to see it because your future actions and efforts will depend on this vision. And based on this vision, they will turn out to be right or wrong.

   - Why do you do what you do? Why do you market these products? Why do you provide these services? Send these questions to your employees, your coworkers, your clients and I can assure you that their responses and feedbacks will have a wonderful effect on you.

2. **Goals**
   - Write down your goals as a business owner, an official, an employee and an individual. Ask the

following questions and answer them in writing.

- How big should your company be?

- What do you want out of your venture?

- How much monthly business do you expect?

- How much annual business do you expect?

- How many employees should you have?

- How much should the company's profit be?

3. **Action**
   - From the time that you have a clear vision for the future, and you have set the strategic objectives for your business, every time there is a need to act, ask yourself the following question: would this action bring me closer to achieving my vision, reaching my goals?

Yes or no?

- If the answer is yes, take action!

- If the answer is no, then do not deal with it any longer.

The easiest way you can reinforce your confidence and overcome the challenge is to approach things with humor and to have a good mentor.

Humor is important. It is one of the best stress reliefs.

# Chapter 13: The Overachiever Procrastinator

The Overachiever Procrastinator is the one who takes on everything without thinking. He will do it all, this is his job, even if it's not.

He is the one who works a lot and takes on even more — often takes on other people's responsibilities and things start to get chaotic. Thus the efficiency of his work is reduced, and he gets little done. He is the one who just goes and goes without a vision, often without a plan.

The space around him is not organized. He takes on more than he can handle. *"Let me play the lion too"*... which leads to complete chaos. He takes on so much that, in the end, he collapses under the weight of it all. It is hard for him to manage things and figure out where to start.

He is characterized by lack of self-control. He does not look at anything or anybody, just goes full steam ahead. Let's do it, whatever it may be and whatever the price. Straining, snarling, and not caring about anybody, then suddenly switching to passive. Low self-control and high impulsivity often lead to procrastination.

He is the ultimate "Multi-tasking Man". (Or woman.)

He has a lot of windows open on his computer, and he is involved with several things at once.

It is said that Napoleon was multi-tasked; he was able to divide his attention in several directions. He managed his surroundings effectively. There was nobody like him! And he ended up in exile on the island of St. Helena.

You should just develop the ability to focus on one particular thing at a time. Concentrate on the task and do it in the shortest time with the greatest efficiency. If you cannot focus on a task for an extended period, it will be tough to be effective.

According to Tony Schwartz, you need about 15 minutes to get into the zone with a task, to get into a rhythm of work. And you need about 15-20 minutes to get out of it too.

During a survey, subjects were asked how long they think they can focus on a particular thing. The vast majority of respondents estimated between 15 and 20 minutes to be able to apply themselves.

So... you basically lose focus by the time you get into it. It is very difficult to be effective without educating and training yourself. Learn discipline to remedy this.

How?

Ask ten powerful questions regarding reaching the goal. We already talked about powerful questions in Chapter 5, Strategies for surviving and overcoming procrastination.

If you recognized yourself based on descriptions in this chapter by identifying the symptoms, you won the right to a 28-day self-education of which you are the trainer and the trainee as well.

Once you have made the decision to replace the bad habit of procrastination with the good habit of activity, take a new sheet of paper. List ten tasks. Attention! Only ten. No more, no less. Don't pick and choose among the multitude of undertaken tasks. Write down the first ten that comes to your mind. Don't think about the order just yet.

Now write down the following thought process as the eleventh task: Starting today, for 28 days I will fully complete the tasks described above. Just what's on my list for the day. Nothing more, nothing less.

Write the eleventh task in a different color or frame it.

When this has been written down, do another task.

Write at least four powerful questions next to each task needing to be done on your list. These questions, even in their wording, should point beyond the task to be done.

For example – if the deadline for an analysis, project, trenching, house painting is the 6th December 2016 at noon, the question *"Why did I complete the analysis, project, trenching, house painting earlier than the deadline?"* is very appropriate.

Back each powerful question relating to a task on your list with positive statements.

For example – *"I have finished with the analysis, project, trenching, house painting earlier than the deadline because...* (of my logical thinking, I purposefully focused on the task performed, I am strong, rested and in good shape, or I created the conditions to get the work done.)"

This is the rule for the first day.

For the next 27 days, you will have to write a maximum of 10 new tasks every day on a new page. Attention! The tasks cannot be repeated. This is the training period, and you should be resolving new issues daily. Be careful not to exceed the requirements. It is also important not to do less than required.

So what is your job?

Make a list of ten tasks daily. Write down four powerful questions per task. Back each question with a positive statement.

Do this for 28 days, every day.

To succeed, you need yourself. Your determination, your decision and your action. You already have the recipe.

Go for it and good luck!

# Chapter 14: Action Plan

You have reached this point, which means you have made a certain decision. You are going to take action and step out of the hole of passivity. You were able to identify what type of procrastinator you are and what steps to take to get procrastination-free days. You just have to practice.

Find your own place in the big picture.

Some good tips can always expand the possibilities. The following are valid points and help emphasize the specific steps for any procrastinator.

If you want to straighten an area of your life, prioritize. When that's done, start working on it.

Deal with one thing at a time. Do not divide your attention and energy - if it hasn't worked so far, it won't in the future either. Learn the new mechanism well and when you can apply it, it will continue to serve you.

Steps:

1. **Focus and visualize what you want**. Many people concentrate on what they want to avoid. They do not want to be overweight anymore. They don't want to be without money and live in poverty. They do not want to cause an accident. The more you want to avoid a roadside tree, the more you focus on it your energy takes you to it. Suddenly you crash into it. Focus on what you want, not what you don't want. Know where you are now and where you are heading.

2. **Make your goal irresistible**. Don't just say to yourself *"Yep. I want to be slim, strong, energetic, or rich..."* Instead use something like: *"I want to burst with energy. I will be more active, I will be stronger, and I will be an example to my kids /my family /my friends as well."*

If you want to take your business to a higher level, it is not enough just to focus. You need to envision your goal so strongly that it makes you take the steps leading to it. Create an image that irresistibly pulls you towards it. A vision is not worth anything if you have to keep kicking yourself to reach it.

Make the goal so irresistible that you immediately want to get started on reaching it, start developing the particular area.

You will experience that your quality of life gets better just because you are excited about where you are headed. Your adrenaline level will rise suddenly, and that's a good feeling.

You can do this with your time (the most valuable thing for a person), your finances, your body or your emotions, etc. Quite simply, if you focus on a clear vision, it will give you the momentum, it will increase your energy levels and as a result, you begin to take action.

3. **Find the best tools**. Find the path to reach your goal, to solve the problem. If it doesn't exist, you will have to build it. Find the starting point. Create it if there isn't one. It is great if you are enthusiastic and focused.

It doesn't matter how focused you are and what you believe if you are using the wrong tools. Wrong strategy or an inappropriate map won't get you closer to your goal either.

I think you need a map and a good mentor. This is crucial. The route may change, and if you learn from the best mentor, his help may shorten the way. When choosing a mentor, good enough is not enough. Choose the best, the one with the best tools for you.

You find the best tools if you imitate someone who is successful at something you want to be successful at. If you emulate someone, you can save time, energy and money.

The system of tools I am using is modeled after successful people, the most successful people. I customized them so the essence is maintained and I learned to use them. If I see someone with outstanding results, who is already successful, why would I want to reinvent the wheel?

Success always leaves lasting traces behind. Find the very best, see what they do and how they do it and copy them. Adapt your own style and monitor the process. Adapt what is already working, instead of doing time-consuming experiments.

4. **Break up your inner conflict**, which often causes the death of action.

   Several forces are fighting with each other when there is an internal conflict. You are the one who can use these forces to your benefit. You need to realize that 80% of success is psychology and the remaining 20% is the "how."

Here comes the lack of "why". Why do you want what you want? Why do you want that particular goal?

You see your goal clearly. You have your tools. Why haven't you reached it yet?

Your internal conflicts are in your way.

You might think that to be successful and make a lot of money is immoral, not spiritual. Maybe you want to be spiritual and in light of this you get in the way of your own financial success.

How can we resolve these inner conflicts and unleash the power of their forces? How do you want to reach your goal if you are flailing around, in a vortex, and the currents are taking you in different directions? How do you resolve this? There is only one way. Identify what is the most important thing for you today.

Do not make a decision based on what you are supposed to do, what happened in your past, and what your belief system is. It is not relevant what your parents or your friends or society think. If you do this, you can still be successful, but you will never be satisfied.

When you manage to identify the conflict, bring the values you represent into harmony with your life. Be in agreement with the things that are most important to you.

You will see, once you are in harmony and resolve your inner conflict action will take place almost by itself. Be open and accept that incredibly gratifying experience of the "aha" moment.

- Dad, is America far yet?
- Yes, son.
- Dad, is America far yet?
- Yes, son.
- Daaad, is America far yet?
- Son, be quiet and keep swimming!

Once you spiritually catch up to your desires and take action, what will happen?

You will reach your goal. If you reach it, that's success. Then celebrate your success. Pass your knowledge on. Help others. Show others what you have and what you have learned.

When you teach others, you constantly share your contentment and the joy that comes with success. Everything starts working in your life.

# Final Words

What's easier? To keep suffering for the rest of your life, put off the solution of your tasks, to delay your things? Or to devote your time to learn a new and useful habit.

In this book, I gave you all the help you need from outsiders.

I took you through the possible causes and consequences of procrastination. I think you could identify with some of the statements.

You read some methods and strategies about overcoming procrastination; now you can use them and implement them to effective practical action.

Why did you buy the book? Answer this question yourself.

Do you want to live a better and more active life? Does it matter on what and how you spend your time? Is it significant with whom? A convenient sloth, cultivating the art of procrastination on an academic level or someone who's out there, does things and is happy? Yes, you could be both – choose one.

The reflector lights are on you! Take a step forward and start!

Twenty-eight days learning and practicing for yourself or a lifetime of further delaying and unfulfillment.
From now on you are also needed to complete the work. Without work, you will not succeed. From here on it is up to you.

Discipline.
Patience.
Endurance.

Nowhere and never existed any book - it's not even this one - which could change anything about you by itself.

Everything you read here is worthless if you do not continue implementing the lessons into action.

You have to decide ... I will do NOW!

I can only help you if you help me to work together to be able to keep my promise I made you at the beginning of this book.

I really believe in you!

*Yours truly,*

*Zoe*

P.S.: If you have questions please don't hesitate to contact me on **zoemckey@gmail.com**. I welcome any kind of constructive opinion as well. I'd like to know how I can help so please share your ideas with me. If you'd like to get helpful tips from me on a weekly basis, visit me at **www.zoemckey.com** and subscribe.

Thank you!

Made in the USA
San Bernardino, CA
12 October 2016